An Addict's Daughter

By: Liberty B. Christmas

Chapter One: My Mom

My mama's name was Wendy Gale, and honestly, she was a gale-force wind in every sense of the word—bold, powerful, and impossible to ignore.

She was born in sunny Long Beach, California, a place of ocean breezes and palm trees, but her life quickly shifted to the quiet rhythms of Raeford, North Carolina, when she was only two years old. She truly found her roots in that small, close-knit town.

Despite being born on the West Coast, she never once claimed it as home—Raeford had her heart, with its dirt roads, simple living, and Southern charm.

She was the youngest of my grandmother's four daughters, a role she played with a mix of sweetness and sass that only the baby of the family could pull off. My grandfather adored her fiercely, and while Wendy was his only biological daughter, he loved all four girls as if they were his own flesh and blood. In his eyes, they were, and he never made a distinction. But as the youngest, she definitely had a way of wrapping everyone around her little finger.

Life wasn't easy—my mama grew up in a family that struggled to make ends meet—but that didn't stop her from being a little bit spoiled.

Wendy always seemed to find a way to get what she wanted. She was charming, and determined, and knew how to work her magic to make things happen.

And though her upbringing might have been humble, she carried herself with the kind of confidence and energy that made her seem larger than life.

My mom had this remarkable way of turning the simplest moments into something special, and even from an early age, she was someone who knew her own mind and wasn't afraid to go after what she wanted.

My mama was only 16 years old when she found out she was pregnant with me. Just a teenager herself, she was suddenly faced with the reality of becoming a mother—something that changes your life in ways you can't fully prepare for, especially at such a young age.

It must have been overwhelming for her, having to grow up so quickly while also learning how to care for a baby. She had to make some hard choices, including dropping out of high school to raise me.

I can picture her as a young girl, standing at that crossroads, trying to figure out how to navigate a world that seemed to be moving so fast.

Being a teen mom myself, I can relate to what she went through. There's a unique kind of stress that comes with trying to balance the chaos of raising a child when you're still growing up yourself. There are moments of doubt, exhaustion, and wondering if you're doing enough—but there are also moments of fierce determination and love that pull you through.

In her late teens, my mama got her first real job working at a pizza place. She started out just trying to make ends meet, but it didn't take long for her to rise through the ranks and eventually become the manager. That says a lot about the kind of person she was—hardworking, determined, and always willing to step up and take charge.

I remember calling her at work all the time, just to hear her voice or to ask her questions that probably weren't all that urgent. Knowing I could always reach her, even when she was busy managing a team and keeping everything running smoothly, gave me a sense of comfort.

When that pizza place eventually closed its doors, it didn't stop her. She moved on to another pizza place and, once again, worked her way up to being the manager. It was like she had this natural talent for leadership, even in the simplest of settings. I imagine she made those places feel like more than just a job for the people who worked with her.

Eventually, she decided to step away from work altogether and she quit working indefinitely.

My mom and dad were together until I was about 5 years old, but my memories of them as a couple are few and hazy. At that age, everything felt like a blur, and the details of their relationship didn't really make much of an impression on me.

I think part of the reason I don't remember much about their time together is that I spent a lot of my early childhood with my grandparents. They were a constant presence in my life, and my most vivid memories from that time aren't of my parents as a couple but of the warmth and love I felt from my grandmother. She had a way of making everything feel safe and comforting, and she was always there to take care of me.

I don't actually remember the moment my parents broke up or any of the emotions that might've surrounded it. Looking back now, I think that's probably because my grandma did such a good job of shielding me from the tension and heartache. She must have worked hard to make sure I felt protected and loved during what was likely a challenging time for my parents.

What I do remember is the aftermath—splitting my time between my mom and dad. I can't say it bothered me too much, though, because even with the changes, I still spent most of my time with my grandma. She was my anchor through it all, and her presence made everything feel a little less uncertain.

It wasn't too long after my parents split up that my grandparents decided to move in with us at my mom's house. That shift made things feel more stable for me. Having them close by meant I didn't have to leave the comfort of my grandmother's care, even as my life changed in other ways.

I remember my mom dating a few men after things ended with my dad. Each time, it felt like a new chapter was starting, though I never really understood much about what was going on back then.

The men she dated were always nice to me—kind and polite—and they seemed to treat my mom well, too, at least as far as I could tell. But eventually, one by one, they just weren't around anymore. It was like they came and went, their presence in our lives disappearing, leaving only vague impressions. I never gave it too much thought as a child; I just accepted it as the way things were.

That is, until my mom met my stepdad.

Not long after my mom and stepdad got together, they had a baby—a little girl—right before my 8th birthday. They named her Victory, and the moment I laid eyes on her, I fell head over heels in love with being a big sister.

There was something magical about holding her tiny little body in my arms and knowing that I had this incredible new role in her life. From the very beginning, I felt this deep bond with her, like it was my job to protect her and cheer her on. Even now, after all these years, I still love being her sister. She's grown into someone so special, and I wouldn't trade her for the world.

Victory isn't just my sister—she's one of the greatest blessings of my life, and I'll always be grateful for the love and joy she's brought into my world

Around the time Victory was about 3 years old, life took a difficult turn for our family. My mom and my stepdad found themselves in trouble with the law. As a child, I didn't fully understand what was happening, but I could sense the tension and stress in our home. The situation escalated, and the ultimate result was that my stepdad was deported back to his home country.

I remember how devastating that was for my mom. The loss of his presence was difficult, and it left a void that wasn't easy to fill. For me, it was confusing and heartbreaking, but for my mom, it was something even deeper—a blow that left her lonely as she tried to figure out how to move forward without him by her side.

At that point, my grandfather had been gone for about two years. Losing him had already been a heavy loss for our family, especially for my grandmother, who had been his partner for so long.

My mother was still grieving his absence when, in the same season of our lives—if I remember correctly, it was wintertime—she received the news that my grandmother had cancer.

It was so overwhelming for her, for my grandmother, and for all of us. It felt like one tragedy after another was hitting us, each wave heavier than the last.

All of these events—the legal troubles, my stepdad's deportation, the loss of my grandfather, and now my grandmother's diagnosis—seemed to take an enormous toll on my mom. She carried so much on her shoulders, and I could see the weight of it in her eyes. It was like life just kept throwing punches, and she had no choice but to take

them and keep going.

Chapter Two: The Addict

I didn't always know that my mother was an addict.

Looking back, I guess it's possible that she wasn't "always" one, or maybe I was just too young and naive to see the signs.

Growing up, I thought she was just like any other mom, but as I got older, certain memories started standing out more clearly.

One of the earliest moments I remember was the time I caught her smoking marijuana. It was such a shocking realization for me as a child.

Up until then, I'd only known her as someone who was constantly puffing on cigarettes, which was something I'd come to accept as part of her daily routine. Cigarettes were her normal; they were a part of her. But marijuana?

That was something different, something she had clearly been hiding from me for a while.

It felt like a part of her world I wasn't supposed to see, and when I did, it shifted my perception of her just a little. At that moment, I started to wonder what else she might be hiding.

There were so many times she would have company over, and I remember being told I wasn't allowed in her room while they were there. The door would stay shut, and I was left to entertain myself.

I hated it—not just because I was a curious kid who wanted to know what was going on, but because I didn't get that much time with her to begin with.

Those moments when she was behind that closed door felt like she was slipping even further away from me.

Then one day, everything changed. I caught her smoking, and it was like this unspoken rule between us shifted.

After that, she stopped hiding it from me. She started letting me come into her room, even when her friends were over.

I'd sit on the bed or in the corner while they passed the blunt around, laughing and talking like it was the most normal thing in the world.

So what if I was only about 10 years old? At the time, I didn't care. All that mattered to me was that I was with my mama. If being in that smoky room meant I got to spend time with her, then I was willing to put up with it.

But even then, deep down, I hated the smell of marijuana. It clung to the air, to her clothes, and to me. Still, I tried to push that aside because, at the end of the day, this was my first real encounter with my mom using illegal drugs. And as much as I tried to normalize it in my mind, something about it didn't sit right with me.

At first, I had no idea that my mom was using drugs (besides marijuana). She was high-functioning, and from the outside, she seemed like a mom who had it all together.

She took whatever the pills are that make you hyper—Percocets, I think—and she also used cocaine. But to me, she was just my mom, and I didn't see the cracks in her façade.

She did things that you wouldn't expect an addict to do, like bringing lunch to school so we could eat together or sending flowers to the front office with little notes for me. Those small gestures made her seem so present, so involved in my life, that even I was convinced she was the perfect parent.

I remember her telling me this one story from when I was in kindergarten. She said she and another mom had gotten high and then joined the kids on the playground during recess, pushing us on the swings like it was the most normal thing in the world.

And the thing is, times really *were* different back then. No one seemed to notice, or if they did, they just looked the other way.

But everything started to change after my stepdad got deported. That moment seemed to mark the beginning of a downward spiral for my mom.

She was struggling to hold it together, and that's when I began to notice more.

She started seeing a psychiatrist, and at first, I thought maybe this would help her cope. But instead, it became the catalyst for something much worse.

The psychiatrist prescribed her Xanax—so much Xanax. At the time, I was about 12 years old, and Victory was just a toddler, around 4. That's when things really started to shift in our home.

My mom began to sleep all the time. She had always been somewhat distant, but now it felt like she wasn't even there anymore.

The psychiatrist prescribed her an almost unbelievable amount of Xanax—240 pills a month. I know it sounds like an impossible number, and honestly, it's shocking even to think about it now.

But it happened.

Every month, she took all 240 pills, or at least whatever she didn't sell. And the effect of that was profound.

By the time I was 13, I had more freedom than I knew what to do with. My mom was so out of it that I could come and go as I pleased, and she never even realized I was gone.

It wasn't the kind of freedom any kid should have. It wasn't liberating; it was lonely.

I remember sneaking out with guys and wandering around, knowing there was no one at home who would check on me, no one who would notice.

At that point, the mother who once brought me lunch and sent flowers seemed like a distant memory. She was there physically, but she wasn't *really* there anymore, and that realization hit me harder than anything.

My mother often claimed to have been diagnosed with a variety of mental health issues.

I put "diagnosed" in quotations because, to this day, I'm not entirely sure if she actually received those diagnoses from a medical professional or if they were self-proclaimed.

She certainly struggled with some very real mental health challenges, and I don't want to diminish or dismiss that.

But at the same time, I truly believe that some of the conditions she said she had were either exaggerated or entirely fabricated.

Whether she convinced herself that she had them, persuaded a psychiatrist to believe her, or simply used them as an excuse to take medication, I'll never know for sure.

I do remember her telling me on one occasion that she would make up wild and outrageous stories to tell the psychiatrist, just to get prescribed more medication.

I think about that often because it makes me question how much of what she claimed was genuine and how much was simply a ploy.

I want to be clear—I am in no way discrediting mental illnesses or downplaying their severity. I understand that mental health conditions are very real and can be debilitating.

I also know that when prescribed and used correctly, medication can be a life-saving tool for those who truly need it.

But in my mother's case, she didn't seem to want the medication for healing—she wanted it for escape, for control, or maybe even for validation.

Looking back, I realize that her misuse of the system wasn't just harmful to herself but also to those around her.

It created an atmosphere of uncertainty, where I could never tell what was real and what was an act. I spent a lot of my life trying to untangle the truth from the fiction, questioning what to believe and what to disregard. In doing so, I learned a hard lesson—mental health is complex, and while some people suffer silently, others might manipulate it to serve their own purposes.

My mother never went back to work.

Instead of working, she relied on renting out rooms in our home to just about anyone who had the money to pay.

There wasn't much of a screening process—if they had the cash, they had a place to stay. That was how we managed to keep the bills paid and the lights on. It wasn't the most stable or safest way to live, but it was the only way she knew how to survive at the time.

One tenant in particular stands out in my memory. He had lived with us for a while, and on multiple occasions, he confided in me that he was feeling homicidal.

It wasn't just passing comments—it was serious. I was young, but even then, I knew that wasn't something to be taken lightly.

I told my mom, hoping she would do something, hoping she would see the danger in allowing someone like that to live under our roof.

But she just brushed it off, dismissing my concerns as if they didn't matter. His money was paying the bills, and as far as she was concerned, that was the priority.

Over the years, many people came and went from our house. Some stayed a short time, others lingered longer. Many of them had their own battles with addiction, their own demons they were fighting.

Our home wasn't just a place to stay—it was a revolving door of troubled souls, a place where people brought their baggage, their struggles, and sometimes, their chaos. And while my mom may have thought she was in control, the truth was, the situation had long since spiraled beyond her grasp.

Eventually, things started falling apart. It became harder and harder to keep the rooms filled. The money stopped coming in the way it once did.

Bills piled up, notices arrived, and before long, reality caught up with her. She lost the house—the one thing that had been keeping her afloat. And with it, she lost everything she had to her name. No savings, no security, no backup plan. Just the weight of years of bad choices and the harsh reality of having nowhere left to turn.

Chapter Three: Losing the Addict for the first time

If I remember correctly, my mom first started claiming to have schizophrenia when I was about 15 years old.

I still recall the way she would talk about it, almost as if it had become part of her identity rather than just a diagnosis.

At the time, I didn't know much about mental illnesses, but as I got older, I became more curious and started reading about schizophrenia from textbooks, medical journals, and online sources.

The more I learned, the more I began to question whether her claim was accurate. Based on the definitions and symptoms I read, her behaviors and experiences didn't seem to align completely with what I understood schizophrenia to be.

Of course, I'm not a doctor or an expert, so my thoughts on the matter are just an uneducated opinion. Still, something about it never quite sat right with me.

Regardless, that was the explanation she consistently gave whenever someone asked about her medications or why she needed them.

It was her go-to response, almost rehearsed as if she had said it a hundred times before.

I sometimes wondered if she truly believed it or if it was just easier to say rather than explain the real reason.

Maybe she had been told this by a doctor at some point, or perhaps it was a label she had adopted over time to make sense of what she was going through.

Either way, schizophrenia became the name she attached to whatever struggles she was facing, and that's how she explained the need for her prescriptions.

When my mother was a child, she had a severe case of strep throat that went untreated, something that, at the time, might have seemed like just another childhood illness. But what started as a simple infection eventually developed into something far more serious—rheumatic fever.

From what I was told, the damage from the fever didn't just go away once she recovered. Instead, it lingered in ways that weren't immediately noticeable, slowly affecting her heart over time.

The inflammation caused by the disease led to scarring and narrowing of her arteries, making it increasingly difficult for her heart to pump blood efficiently.

At least, that's how it was all explained to me as I tried to understand what was happening to her.

By the time she was 32 years old, she received a life-changing diagnosis: congestive heart failure.

It was a terrifying realization, not only for her but for all of us who loved her.

But despite how serious it was, there was still hope. She wasn't at a point of no return—she was still young enough that if she made significant changes to her lifestyle, she could potentially slow the progression of the disease and give herself more years with us.

I remember sitting in the doctor's office, the moment burned into my memory, as the doctor laid it all out.

He made it very clear that if my mother didn't start taking her health seriously—if she didn't quit smoking, if she didn't make better choices—she wouldn't live to see my sister graduate high school.

The weight of those words hit hard. My sister was only eight years old at the time, still just a child.

The thought that she might have to go through life without our mother by the time she reached her teenage years was almost too much to process.

It was a warning, a wake-up call, and a desperate plea all rolled into one. But whether or not my mother truly understood the gravity of it, or if she felt capable of making those changes, was something I wasn't sure of.

After spending some time in the hospital following her initial diagnosis, my mom made a promise to me and my sister—one that, at the time, I so badly wanted to believe.

She looked us in the eyes and swore that, at the very least, she was going to stop smoking cigarettes. It felt like a turning point, a moment where she was acknowledging the seriousness of her condition and choosing to fight for her health, for us.

I held onto those words, hoping they meant she was ready to make the changes that could give her more time with us.

But later that same day, reality came crashing down in a way I'll never forget. I walked into the room and saw her, cigarette in hand, desperately trying to hide it from me. In her panic, she moved too quickly and ended up burning a hole straight through her blanket.

I stood there for a moment, watching the embers smolder, watching the way she scrambled to cover up what she had done, and something inside me shifted.

That was the moment I knew—we had lost our mom.

Not in the physical sense, not yet. But the mother I had known, the mother who could take control and fight for her future, was slipping away.

That didn't mean I lost hope entirely.

I still wanted to believe there was a chance, that something might change, that she might wake up one day and find the strength to fight.

But I also knew, in that instant, that things weren't going to be as simple as I had hoped.

My mother was still there, but she wasn't the same.

She was battling something deeper than just a physical illness—something that made it impossible for her to follow through on the promises she made, no matter how much she might have wanted to.

And that realization was one of the hardest things I ever had to come to terms with.

Chapter Four: Loving the Addict

My sister and I loved our mom deeply—more than words could ever express.

She had this natural way of making people feel comfortable as if they belonged, and she carried a kindness that drew others in.

One of the things we loved most about her was her sense of humor.

She could turn even the toughest moments into something lighthearted with a well-timed joke, and her laughter was contagious.

She always talked about standing up for those who couldn't stand up for themselves, teaching us that strength wasn't just about fighting for yourself—it was about fighting for others too.

As much as we adored her, we also longed for change.

We wanted more for her.

We wanted to see her rise above the struggles that weighed her down.

We wanted to see her sober, to see her live the life we knew she deserved.

We dreamed of the day she would finally break free from the things that held her back and step into the fullness of who she was meant to be. But life doesn't always unfold the way we hope.

Sometimes, the battles we pray to see won don't end the way we imagined.

Despite our love for her, despite our deepest wishes, things didn't exactly go our way.

When I was 16, I reached a breaking point. I had spent so many years hoping my mom would change, but things only seemed to get worse.

She slept all the time, completely detached from what was happening around her, and I was left feeling like I had to navigate life without a mother.

I needed her—I needed guidance, support, and love—but instead, I felt like I was raising myself.

Our home had fallen into complete disarray. It was beyond messy; it was unspeakably dirty, a place that no child should have had to live in.

I was exhausted from trying to manage it all, from hoping she'd wake up one day and decide to take care of things, but that day never came.

Eventually, I realized I couldn't keep living like that, so I made a decision that no teenager should have to make.

I picked up the phone and called Social Services.

I told them everything—how she wasn't taking care of the house, how she wasn't taking care of us, how I desperately needed something to change.

The response was immediate.

My sister and I were removed from our home, and for a brief moment, I felt a strange mix of relief and guilt. Relief that someone had finally stepped in, but guilt because, deep down, I still just wanted my mom.

It took her about two to three months to get clean enough to get us back.

I remember feeling hopeful, thinking maybe this was the wake-up call she needed.

Maybe this was the turning point.

But as soon as we returned home, it was as if nothing had changed. She slipped right back into her old habits, and to make things worse, she resented me for what I had done.

She didn't see my call as an act of desperation from a child who needed her mother—she saw it as a betrayal.

She talked badly about me, both to me and to others, making me feel like I was the villain in a story where all I ever wanted was for her to be the hero.

Instead of making things better, it just made my life harder. I thought I was doing the right thing, but in the end, I was left feeling more alone than ever.

That same year, I started working a full-time job, trying to build something for myself—some stability, some independence.

It wasn't easy balancing work, school, and everything else going on at home, but I was determined.

I worked long hours, often coming home completely drained, but at least I had something to show for it.

I had been carefully saving every dollar I could, tucking it away in the top drawer of my dresser. I wanted to buy a car.

Then, one day, after working a grueling 15-hour shift, I came home to find all of my money gone. Every last bit of it.

My heart sank.

My brand-new laptop, which would have been the first thing a real thief would grab, was still sitting right there on my bed.

The only thing missing was the money.

The money that only a handful of people even knew existed, and one of those people was my mom.

She called the cops and reported it as if someone had broken into our home.

She played the part, acting shocked and upset, but something about it just didn't sit right with me. The details didn't add up, and deep down, I couldn't shake the feeling that I already knew what had happened.

I'm not saying conclusively that my mom stole it, but let's be real—what are the odds?

Not long after that, my life took another unexpected turn—I got pregnant.

At just 16, I was overwhelmed with emotions, unsure of what the future would hold. But before I even had time to process it all, I was hit with devastating news.

At five weeks, my baby had no heartbeat. I miscarried.

I was heartbroken, but during my pain, something unexpected happened.

During the process of confirming my miscarriage, the doctor found something that shouldn't have been there—a massive cyst growing inside my fallopian tube.

At first, it was just a concern, something that needed to be monitored. But as the weeks passed, the concern turned into something much more serious. It took months of tests, scans, and uncertainty before they finally determined that I needed surgery.

By then, the cyst had grown to an astonishing nine pounds. Nine pounds of something that shouldn't have been there, something that could have killed me if it had gone unnoticed.

That's when I realized—God had been with me the whole time.

As painful as it was to lose my baby, that pregnancy led to the discovery of the cyst.

If I hadn't gotten pregnant at 16, I might not have survived to tell this story.

It was a hard lesson in faith, in trusting that even in my darkest moments, God was still working things together for my good. He knew what He was doing.

But while God was with me, my mother wasn't.

She wasn't there for the appointments.

She wasn't there for the scans.

She wasn't there when I faced the reality of surgery.

Even as I lay in a hospital bed, vulnerable and afraid, she was absent.

And that absence cut deep.

No matter how much I tried to convince myself that I didn't need her, the truth was—I did. I needed my mom.

But where she lacked, God provided.

My Nana stepped in and became my rock.

She was there through every single step, holding my hand when I needed strength, and reassuring me when fear crept in.

I thank God for her every day because, without her, I don't know how I would have made it through. But even with all her love and support, it didn't completely fill the void.

It didn't take away the ache of knowing the one person who should have been there—the one person I needed most—chose not to be.

The winter after I turned 17 was brutal, not just because of the cold, but because of the reality of the life my sister and I were living.

The heater in our house needed gas, and my mom refused to pay for it.

I don't know if it was out of neglect, stubbornness, or something else entirely, but the result was the same—we were left to fend for ourselves in a freezing house.

My sister and I shared a room, and we did what we could to stay warm. We layered on clothes, huddled under blankets, and tried to convince ourselves that it wasn't as bad as it felt.

But one particular night proved just how unbearable things had become.

Before going to bed, we left a glass of ice water on the nightstand. When we woke up the next morning, instead of the ice melting overnight, there was more ice in the water than when we had gone to sleep.

The house was so cold that the water had frozen even more as we slept.

That was it for me.

I looked at my sister and told her, pack your stuff. We're going to stay with Nana.

There was no hesitation, no second-guessing. I had finally reached the point where I knew—I couldn't do this anymore.

I refused to keep pretending that things would get better, that my mother would suddenly step up and take care of us.

That was the last night I ever stayed at my mom's house.

When I was 18, I gave birth to my oldest son.

It was one of the most life-changing moments I had ever experienced.

For the first time, I wasn't just responsible for myself—I had a tiny human who depended on me completely.

And surprisingly, my mom was there.

She was present for the birth, and she even cut the umbilical cord.

In that moment, it felt like maybe, just maybe, things could be different. She told me she wanted to be there for us, that she wanted to be involved in my son's life.

I wanted to believe her.

I needed to believe her.

But just like so many times before, her promises didn't last.

That brief glimpse of hope was short-lived.

By then, she was pretty much homeless, and despite everything we had been through, I still wanted to help her. I asked her to come stay with us, offering her a chance to have some stability, to be a part of our lives.

But I had one condition—there would be rules. Rules including no cigarettes around my baby, and no running in and out of the house at all hours of the night.

They were simple rules, I thought.

But to her, it was too much.

She refused.

She said she couldn't stay if it meant following those rules.

It was devastating—not just for me, but for my sister too. We had spent our entire lives wanting her to choose us, to choose family over everything else.

And once again, she showed us where her priorities were.

As much as it hurt, it was also eye-opening.

I had just become a mother myself, and I knew without a doubt that I would do anything for my child.

That's what a mother is supposed to do.

Yet, here was mine, walking away from me and her grandson because she wasn't willing to make even the smallest sacrifices.

That moment solidified something in me.

I realized that I couldn't keep chasing after her love, hoping she would one day be the mother I needed.

I had my own child now, and my focus had to be on being the kind of mom that he deserved. Even though it broke my heart, I had to let her go.

At that time, my mom technically still had custody of my sister, even though in reality, my sister was with me the majority of the time—probably about 90% of the time.

I did everything I could to provide a stable home for her, but my mom still had control in certain ways.

Whenever she got mad at me, she would make my sister leave and stay with her, dragging her along to random houses, and bouncing from place to place.

It was like my sister was being used as a pawn, and no matter how hard I tried to shield her from the chaos, my mom still had the legal power to pull her away.

One day, I had to pick up my 10-year-old sister at the top of a dirt road.

When I got there, she was standing with some grown man I had never seen before.

My stomach dropped.

I didn't know who he was, what his intentions were, or what my little sister had been exposed to while she was there.

I was done.

That was the final straw.

The very next day, I called Social Services.

I told them everything.

I refused to let my sister be put in harm's way any longer.

She deserved stability.

She deserved safety.

She deserved better.

They granted me full custody, and from that point on, I raised my sister—with the unwavering help of our Nana.

It wasn't easy stepping into that role at such a young age, but there was no question in my mind—I would do whatever it took to give her the life our mother never would.

I became more than just a big sister. I became her protector, her provider, and, in many ways, the mother figure she needed.

And yet, despite everything, despite all the hurt, the disappointment, and the abandonment, we still loved our mom.

We still held onto hope.

No matter how many times she let us down, we still wanted to see her change.

We still longed for the day she would finally choose us.

But as much as we wished for that, we also knew that we couldn't keep waiting.

We had to move forward, even if she never did.

Chapter Five: Pushing for Recovery

As time went by, keeping up with my mother became more and more difficult.

She was always drifting, never staying in one place for too long.

We never really knew where she was, who she was with, or how to get in contact with her. It was like she existed in a world of her own, separate from us, always just out of reach.

When we did manage to see her, it was usually because we had tracked her down or because she had momentarily resurfaced.

Whenever that happened, we did what we could to help.

We would bring her clothes, food, or anything else we thought she might need.

No matter how much she had hurt us, no matter how unreliable she had been, she was still our mother. And we still cared.

One thing I can say is that she always made an effort to reach out on our birthdays.

No matter how distant she was the rest of the year, she found a way to call or see us when that day came around.

It was something small, but in a way, it meant everything. It was proof that, even in her chaos, she still thought about us.

And sometimes, there were these brief windows of time—maybe a month or two—where she would stay in contact more regularly.

Those were the moments that made us hope again, and made us think maybe things were changing.

But they never lasted.

Just as quickly as she had returned, she would disappear again, leaving us with nothing but questions and a familiar ache in our hearts.

Still, no matter how much time passed, no matter how unpredictable she was, we never stopped wanting her to be okay.

We never stopped wishing for her to come back to us—not just physically, but truly be the mother we had always needed.

But deep down, we knew that wanting something didn't make it happen.

And loving someone didn't mean they would change.

The biggest problem our mother had was realizing she had a problem.

No matter how bad things got, no matter how many times she lost everything, she never truly admitted that anything was wrong with her.

She always had a reason, an excuse, or someone else to blame. In her mind, she wasn't struggling—she was just doing what she had to do to get by.

She told us she self-medicated for her mental conditions, but that explanation never gave us much comfort.

Maybe she believed it, maybe it was true, but either way, it didn't change the damage it caused. It didn't change the way it stole her from us, the way it took a mother away from her children.

We wanted to help her more than anything.

We wanted to see her healthy, stable, and living the life we knew she was capable of.

But how do you help someone who doesn't want to be helped?

How do you save someone who refuses to admit they're drowning?

The truth is, we couldn't.

And that was one of the hardest things to accept.

No matter how much we loved her, no matter how badly we wanted to fix things, change had to be something she wanted. And for as long as we could remember, she just…

didn't.

That was the painful reality we had to face.

We could love her.

We could hope for her.

But we couldn't save her.

Only she could do that.

And until she was ready to see that for herself, there was nothing we could do but watch from a distance, waiting for the day she might finally choose a different path.

Chapter Six: Drained

On December 27, 2022, everything changed.

We got a call from the hospital—one that we had always feared but never truly prepared for.

They told us we needed to come in immediately and asked for all the family to be there.

That alone told us it was serious.

When we arrived, we were met by the doctors, and the weight of their words hit us like a ton of bricks.

My mother's arteries had become so dangerously narrow from years of neglecting her health that her heart was barely functioning.

They didn't expect her to live past three days.

Hearing those words felt unreal.

After everything—after all the chaos, the distance, the hoping, the disappointments—this was how it was going to end?

We had spent so many years wishing she would get better, holding on to hope that one day she would choose a different life.

But now, there were no more second chances. No more time to wait for change. No more space for "maybe someday."

The life she had lived, the choices she had made, had finally caught up with her.

As we sat there, absorbing the reality of it all, a thousand emotions ran through us—sadness, frustration, regret, love.

No matter what had happened in the past, she was still our mother. And now, we were about to lose her.

After that meeting with the doctors, they moved my mom to a hospice house, where they began end-of-life care.

It was surreal, watching everything unfold, knowing that we were preparing to say goodbye.

But despite the doctors' predictions, she did something none of us expected—she kept living.

Not only did she survive those three days they had given her, but she held on long enough to see my birthday on January 27th and my sister's on January 20th.

Her decline seemed to slow, almost as if time had paused. The prayers from my entire church were making a difference—because, against all odds, she wasn't getting worse.

In fact, she was doing better.

Better enough that the medical team started to reconsider.

They told us that she might actually have a chance at living. It was a glimmer of hope in the middle of what had felt like a final chapter.

On February 5th, I took her from the hospice house and brought her back to the hospital so she could receive proper care.

During the drive from the hospice house to the hospital, I received a phone call saying that my oldest son's father had passed away.

I don't think I will ever forget that day, the weight of it, the way the emotions were all over the place in more ways than one.

In just 24 hours, I had gone from holding onto hope for my mother to mourning another devastating loss.

It was too much, too fast, and I could barely process it.

all.

After going back to the hospital, Mom's situation became even more uncertain.

She was constantly moving from place to place.

At this point, I had three kids to take care of. My home was already full, stretched to its limits. One of my children was even sleeping in the living room because there just wasn't enough space.

As much as I wanted to help my mom, I simply had nowhere to put her.

And even if I did, there was another issue I couldn't ignore—her boyfriend.

He had never been good for her, and she refused to leave him alone.

I knew that if she came to stay with me, he would be part of the equation.

And that was something I couldn't allow in my home, not with my kids there.

I had to protect them, no matter how much it hurt to tell my mom no.

She had the option to stay in a nursing home, a place where she would receive the care she needed.

But she declined.

She didn't want to be there, didn't want to accept that this was where life had brought her.

And so, she continued on, drifting from place to place, while I carried the heavy weight of knowing that, as much as I loved her, there was only so much I could do.

Even after everything, my mom continued to use drugs. It was a cycle that never seemed to end, no matter how much we prayed, no matter how many times she had been on the brink of death.

Three more times in 2023, she found herself back in the hospital, and each time, they told us she wouldn't live long. And yet, somehow, she kept pulling through. She lived.

Of course, we were still praying. We had never stopped.

I tried so hard to convince my mom to get clean, to break free from everything and everyone that was dragging her down.

I wanted so badly for her to see that she was worth more than the life she had been living. That there was still time to turn things around.

But wanting change for someone doesn't mean they'll want it for themselves.

After her third hospital stay that year, my aunt stepped in and took my mom into her home.

For the first time in what felt like forever, my mom was away from the drugs.

She was far from the people who had only ever caused her more pain.

It was a small victory, and I clung to it. But even though she was finally in a better environment, her health was still fragile.

Years of neglect had taken their toll.

I was working a lot, juggling my job and raising my kids, and my aunt lived far away. I could only get to her about once a month, which weighed on me, but I was grateful knowing she was in a safer place.

Unfortunately, it wasn't long before a new challenge emerged.

This time, it wasn't drugs that altered her mind—it was the medications she was prescribed for her condition.

The very thing that was supposed to help her was making her delusional, and it became more than my aunt could handle. She was older herself, and caring for my mom was becoming overwhelming.

Six months had passed since my mom had left her old life behind, and then, she got really sick again.

My aunt had no choice but to take her back to the hospital.

It was yet another turning point, another moment where we didn't know what would happen next. And all we could do was wait.

We were so tired.

It felt like we had been living in a constant state of fear, exhaustion, and heartbreak.

The long drives, the endless hospital visits, the gut-wrenching moments where we thought we were losing her—it was an emotional rollercoaster that never seemed to stop.

Every time the doctors told us she wouldn't make it, it was like experiencing her death over and over again.

And every time she pulled through, we were left trying to process the whiplash of relief and dread, knowing we'd likely have to face it all again soon.

We wanted to have hope, to believe that maybe this time would be different. But after so many years of watching her suffer, of watching her choose self-destruction over healing, it was hard to keep holding on.

The weight of it all was unbearable.

Loving someone who refuses to help themselves is one of the hardest things in the world. And no matter how much we prayed, no matter how much we wanted her to change, we were powerless to save her.

We were just… so tired.

When it was time for Mom to be discharged from the hospital, the question of where she would go came up again.

She couldn't go back to my aunt's house—my aunt had done all she could, but it had become too much for her to handle. The nursing home was still an option, a place where she could receive the care she needed, but she still refused.

And then she called me.

I knew what she was going to ask before the words even left her mouth. She wanted me to take her to the drug house.

I refused.

The conversation quickly turned heated. We exchanged some unfriendly words—words filled with frustration, hurt, and years of built-up pain.

She was angry at me for not giving in.

I was angry at her for even asking.

But before I ended the call, I made sure she heard one thing loud and clear.

"I love you, but I will not enable your behavior."

And I meant it.

I had spent my entire life trying to save her, trying to help her, trying to be the daughter who held everything together. But at some point, I had to draw a line.

I had my own children to protect, my own life to take care of. And as much as I loved her, I couldn't be the one to drive her deeper into destruction.

It was one of the hardest things I've ever had to do—choosing to love her from a distance instead of enabling her up close. But I knew, deep down, it was the only choice I had left.

Chapter Seven: Losing the Addict the Last Time

October 20, 2023—just one week after my mom had left the hospital—I got a call that I had always feared but somehow still wasn't ready for.

It was the hospital.

She had a heart attack. Her heart had stopped.

She had already been in the ER for severe swelling in her body when it happened. They managed to revive her, but when they called me, she was sedated, and unresponsive.

The weight of it all hit me instantly.

I left work that Friday and rushed to the hospital.

When I got there, the doctors laid everything out for me.

They planned to run tests over the weekend to check for brain function, to see if there was still hope.

And then, they hit me with something I wasn't expecting— they told me she had meth in her system and that it was likely the trigger for the heart attack.

I had always known my mom did hard drugs, but I never knew she had done *meth*.

Hearing it out loud, having it confirmed like that, was a gut punch I wasn't prepared for.

As much as I had seen and experienced with her over the years, this still felt like a new kind of heartbreak.

It was like every time I thought I understood the full scope of her choices, there was always more—always something else lurking in the shadows.

And now, those choices had led her here.

The drugs, combined with her already failing heart, had finally caught up with her.

Her boyfriend was there, and we never got along.

He had always encouraged her addiction, always kept her tied to the very thing that was killing her.

I couldn't stand to be in the same room with him, knowing the role he had played in her downfall.

So that weekend, I didn't stay at the hospital. But I called. Over and over. Checking for updates, hoping for some kind of miracle.

By Sunday, they took her off sedation. But she didn't wake up.

The tests confirmed what I had feared—there was no brain activity.

She was gone in every way that mattered.

As if that wasn't enough, they also found a mass on her lung.

They believed it was cancer.

Another blow, another unanswered question that no longer mattered because no amount of treatment could bring her back.

I scheduled a meeting with the doctors for Monday afternoon to discuss what came next.

I had to face the reality that, this time, she wasn't going to beat the odds.

This time, she wasn't going to come back.

Monday morning, around 10 a.m., I was sitting at my desk at work when my phone rang.

It was the doctor.

My heart sank before I even answered.

She had another heart attack. Her heart had stopped again.

And once again, they brought her back.

But this time, there was a different tone in the doctor's voice—one that told me we were running out of time.

They didn't know how long they could keep her alive.

Those words echoed in my mind, making it hard to breathe.

I needed my sister. She had to know.

I called her once. No answer.

I called again. And again. And again. Still nothing.

Panic set in.

I couldn't do this without her.

I texted her best friend, hoping she was nearby. When that didn't work, I somehow managed to track down her boss' number and called.

Finally, I got an answer—she had left her phone somewhere.

I didn't have time to wait. I jumped in my car and drove straight to her.

Without hesitation, we went straight to the hospital.

I didn't know what we would walk into when we got there, but I knew one thing for certain—this time, we had to be there.

We arrived at the hospital around 11 a.m. My heart was pounding, my mind racing, knowing that this moment—the one I had dreaded my entire life—was finally here.

We started making calls to close family, letting them know what was happening.

Two of my aunts made it to the hospital to be with us, standing beside us in the hardest moment we had ever faced.

For years, I had told myself that if it ever came to this—if there were no other options—I would do the right thing.

I wouldn't prolong her suffering.

I wouldn't let her stay trapped in a body that was failing her.

I had always said I would consent to a DNR, that I wouldn't let her be in pain just so we could hold on a little longer.

And now, here we were.

The doctors laid out the choices in front of us. We could pull her off life support, or we could wait for what they said would be inevitable—another heart attack, one they didn't believe she would survive.

I thought I had been prepared for this moment, but the reality of it hit differently.

I couldn't bring myself to pull the plug.

As much as I knew it was coming, as much as I had told myself I would do the right thing, the finality of it made my hands shake, my heart ache.

Then, something happened that shattered any hesitation I had left.

She started having seizure after seizure.

Each one shook her fragile body, and we just stood there, helpless, watching.

My sister asked the doctor the one question I wasn't ready to hear the answer to.

"Can she feel this?"

The doctor hesitated, then answered. "She likely can."

That was it.

That was all I needed to hear.

I broke.

I began to weep.

I couldn't bear the thought of her suffering any longer.

I had spent my entire life watching her struggle, and now, in what was likely her final moments, she was still in pain. I had to let her go.

Through my tears, I told them to turn off the machines.

It was the hardest decision I have ever made, but in that moment, I knew—I had to stop the suffering.

I had to let my mom rest.

On October 23, 2023, at 1:33 p.m., my mother took her final breath.

She passed away with a small wooden cross in her hand, the same one she had always carried with her.

After everything—after all the struggles, the pain, the chaos—she left this world holding onto something that symbolized faith.

Three months later, my sister graduated high school.

Chapter 8: More than an Addict

Mom was a beautiful soul—flawed, yes, but deeply human, deeply her.

No matter what, she loved people in a way that was real and undeniable.

She had a way of making people laugh, of bringing light into a room, even when her own life felt dark.

She always wanted to have fun, to enjoy the little things, to make life feel lighter than it really was.

She loved country music, and she loved it loud. She didn't just listen to it—she felt it. She'd turn it all the way up, windows down, singing along like nobody was watching.

She had a passion for thrift shopping and yard sales, hunting for little treasures in places most people overlooked. There was something about the thrill of the find, the nostalgia of old things, the stories they carried, that made her light up.

She had her favorite little indulgences—Red Bulls and Coca-Colas. It didn't matter what time of day it was, she always had one in hand.

At every birthday party, no matter whose it was, she made sure there was a huge fruit tray. It was her thing, her tradition, her way of adding her own touch to the celebration.

She loved doing her hair and makeup, getting all dolled up, looking cute. No matter what was going on in her life, she still wanted to feel pretty. She still cared about those little things that made her feel her.

She loved saying "Hey boo", like it was her signature greeting. It was just one of those little quirks that made her her.

She loved helping people—even when she didn't have much to give, she still found a way to show kindness.

She loved sentimental things, the little keepsakes that held meaning, the things that told a story.

She loved arts and crafts, making things with her hands, and bringing creativity into the world in her own unique way.

And one thing she absolutely hated? Onions. In any way, shape, or form. It didn't matter how they were cooked or hidden—she wanted no part of them.

But most of all, beyond the addiction, beyond the struggles,

beyond the choices that stole so much from her…

She was my mom.

And I love her.

And I miss her.

Made in the USA
Columbia, SC
06 April 2025